Gratitude 365

First Published 2023

© Celeste Jensen. 2023

This

Gratitude Journal

belongs to:

_____

_____

_____

Introduction

I'm delighted you've found your way to this gratitude journal. My greatest hope is that it will become your guide toward a more fulfilled and joyful life.

When I first started cultivating a gratitude practice, I was amazed at the lasting and meaningful changes it made to my life. Incorporating gratitude activities into my life helped me feel more satisfied and content.

And now you can do the same. The exercises and prompts in this journal are carefully designed to help you to grow a lasting gratitude practice. With consistent use you'll gain a more positive perspective on life.

What exactly is gratitude?

Gratitude is being appreciative of the people, events, things and experiences that we have in our lives. When you cultivate gratitude in your life, I guarantee you will immediately start to feel joyful, content and happy. As you continue with gratitude practices over a longer period of time, you'll also start to notice you are able to cope with challenging situations better, you feel healthier, you become more resilient and you feel greater optimism.

By developing a personal practice for gratitude, you will start to see that gratitude is a powerful tool. The key is to make this practice a habit so that being grateful each day becomes easy.

This journal will walk you step by step through gratitude processes which are scientifically proven to make you healthier, have better relationships, help you sleep better, and improve your self-esteem.

Celeste x

How to Use This Journal

Creating a gratitude habit is the best way to welcoming gratitude into your life. However, it can be challenging and difficult to stick with at first. Remind yourself that the more you do it, the easier it will get. These steps will help you to use this book to the fullest:

1 Sit comfortably and take slow, deep breaths.

2 Choose a gratitude prompt (these have not been numbered on purpose, this way you can choose a prompt that fits best for your day.)

3 Let the question sit in your mind for a minute. There's no rush to answer right away.

4 Write down your response.

5 Soak up the good feelings that come as a result. This allows you to maximize on the positive effects of gratitude journaling.

Additional Activities

Practicing gratitude can extend beyond a journal. To help you find additional ways to incorporate gratitude into your life, I have included activities in addition to the journal prompts. I encourage to try these activities and see which of them resonate with you the most. Keep those activities in your back pocket to use at times when you need an extra boost of gratitude.

The Benefits of Gratitude

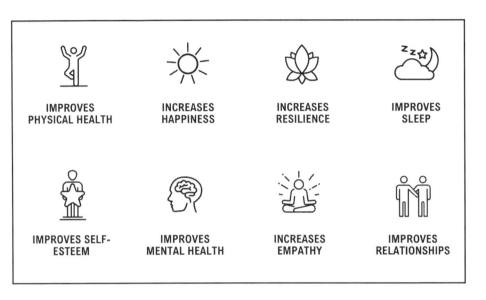

IMPROVES PHYSICAL HEALTH	**INCREASES HAPPINESS**	**INCREASES RESILIENCE**	**IMPROVES SLEEP**
IMPROVES SELF-ESTEEM	**IMPROVES MENTAL HEALTH**	**INCREASES EMPATHY**	**IMPROVES RELATIONSHIPS**

Gratitude is a simple practice that has multiple benefits.

Gratitude is a simple practice that has multiple benefits. Scientific research has shown that people who practice gratitude tend to be more optimistic and happier with their lives than those who don't have a consistent practice. Moreover, those people who show gratitude daily, experience improved physical and mental health. Another benefit of cultivating a gratitude practice is that it strengthens your resilience and ability to cope with stress. Additionally, being grateful can make you feel more generous, compassionate and forgiving which helps you form good relationships and therefore helps you to avoid feelings of loneliness and isolation.

The way that you incorporate gratitude into your day may look very different to another person's gratitude routine. Essentially, it is a personal choice and involves listening to your own body and understanding exactly what it is you need. There are many different ways to focus on gratitude including writing in a journal, creating a gratitude box or jar, using gratitude trackers or simply spending time thinking about the things for which you are grateful.

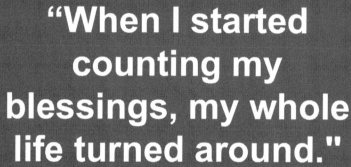

"When I started counting my blessings, my whole life turned around."
Willie Nelson

How could gratitude have a positive impact on a current situation or challenge?

_____

_____

_____

_____

_____

_____

What is an item you are thankful to have?

_____

_____

_____

_____

_____

Describe a family tradition, seperate from holiday traditions, that you are thankful for.

_____

_____

_____

_____

_____

_____

What is one positive thing you have said to yourself today?

_____

_____

_____

_____

_____

_____

Identify some things about you that are good.

_____

_____

_____

_____

_____

Reflect on a person who has always been there for you.

_____

_____

_____

_____

_____

_____

What is the hardest thing you have had to do? What positive outcomes did it lead to?

_____

_____

_____

_____

_____

_____

What is an achievement you are proud of from your past?

_____

_____

_____

_____

_____

_____

Write about someone you have never met but has enriched your life in some way.

_____

_____

_____

_____

_____

_____

What has been the best thing about being the age that you are?

_____

_____

_____

_____

_____

What is an activity you enjoy? Express gratitude for that activity.

_____

_____

_____

_____

_____

What is something consistently burdensome about your life that makes you a stronger person?

_____

_____

_____

_____

_____

What makes you feel confident? Fierce? Bold? Take a moment to be grateful for those things.

_____

_____

_____

_____

_____

_____

Write about a time you were grateful for something a loved one did for you.

_____

_____

_____

_____

_____

_____

Describe a personal strength you are grateful to possess.

_____

_____

_____

_____

_____

List 5 things you will stop to notice and appreciate in the next 24 hours.

_____

_____

_____

_____

_____

List three people you admire and why they inspire you.

_____

_____

_____

_____

_____

What is a talent or skill you are thankful to have?

_____

_____

_____

_____

_____

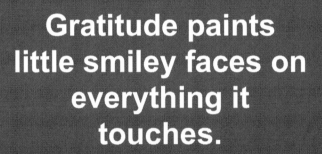

Gratitude paints little smiley faces on everything it touches.

Richelle E. Goodrich

What non-tangible joy can you appreciate today? (a smile, wisdom, etc.)

_____
_____
_____
_____
_____
_____

Describe a piece of advice that positively influenced your life.

_____
_____
_____
_____
_____
_____

Write about a teacher, coach, or supervisor that has helped you in your life.

_____
_____
_____
_____
_____
_____

When you look up at the stars at night, what do you think about?

_____

_____

_____

_____

_____

_____

Write about your favorite animal and why you love it.

_____

_____

_____

_____

_____

_____

Write down some necessities in your life, such as food or shelter, you are grateful for.

_____

_____

_____

_____

_____

_____

What is something you enjoy now that you did not used to?

_____

_____

_____

_____

_____

Describe a favorite piece of clothing or accessory.

_____

_____

_____

_____

_____

Who is someone you are thankful for who is not in your life anymore?

_____

_____

_____

_____

_____

Even on your worst days, what is one thing you can be grateful for?

_____

_____

_____

_____

_____

_____

Write about something beautiful that moved you to tears.

_____

_____

_____

_____

_____

_____

When did something wonderful happen unexpectedly?

_____

_____

_____

_____

_____

_____

What is a good memory you made recently with one of your friends or family members?

_____

_____

_____

_____

_____

Reflect on a time where you felt grateful for your ability to adapt.

_____

_____

_____

_____

_____

What are 10 items you own that make your life easier (technology, appliances, etc.)?

_____

_____

_____

_____

_____

Do you think someone wakes up feeling grateful? Or do you have to practice?

_____

_____

_____

_____

_____

List 5 things in your bedroom that you are grateful for.

_____

_____

_____

_____

_____

Write about a holiday tradition and why it's important to you.

_____

_____

_____

_____

_____

What parts of your life are you happy about?

_____

_____

_____

_____

_____

Write about a favorite book and why you are grateful for it.

_____

_____

_____

_____

_____

Express gratitude for whatever gets you from place to place.

_____

_____

_____

_____

_____

When is a time that gratitude made your life better?

_____

_____

_____

_____

_____

_____

Reflect on a personal breakthrough you have had.

_____

_____

_____

_____

_____

_____

Describe a favorite vacation or travel experience.

_____

_____

_____

_____

_____

_____

What relationship (past or present) has taught you something about gratitude?

_____

_____

_____

_____

_____

When did someone smile or laugh because of you? How did that make you feel?

_____

_____

_____

_____

_____

What is your strongest life value? How are values a positive piece of your life?

_____

_____

_____

_____

_____

_____

"I think gratitude is a big thing. It puts you in a place where you're humble."

Andra Day

Express gratitude for things that make you feel alive.

_____

_____

_____

_____

_____

Write about a cultural experience that broadened your horizons.

_____

_____

_____

_____

_____

What is something positive about today's weather?

_____

_____

_____

_____

_____

Identify another culture that you admire. Write down three ways you are grateful for that culture.

_____

_____

_____

_____

_____

_____

Who is a local business owner you admire, and why?

_____

_____

_____

_____

_____

_____

Write about a favorite quote that inspires you.

_____

_____

_____

_____

_____

_____

What is a recent experience that you are glad to have had?

_____

_____

_____

_____

_____

Name one time you felt uncomfortable with change. After this change, how did your life improve?

_____

_____

_____

_____

_____

What did you like about growing up?

_____

_____

_____

_____

_____

List something you love and look forward to about each spring.

_____

_____

_____

_____

_____

_____

List three characteristics you appreciate in your closest friend.

_____

_____

_____

_____

_____

_____

List three acts of kindness you can perform for others. How do simple acts of kindness enrich your life?

_____

_____

_____

_____

_____

_____

List something you love and look forward to about each fall.

_____

_____

_____

_____

_____

_____

Name a superhero or character you admire and why.

_____

_____

_____

_____

_____

What is one part of your life that you would not trade for anything?

_____

_____

_____

_____

_____

_____

List something you love and look forward to about each summer.

_____

_____

_____

_____

_____

_____

What is a charity or cause you are thankful for, and why?

_____

_____

_____

_____

_____

_____

Who is the person in your life that you will call in an emergency?

_____

_____

_____

_____

_____

_____

List something you love and look forward to about each winter.

_____

_____

_____

_____

_____

What was the most enjoyable part of your childhood?

_____

_____

_____

_____

_____

Write a thank-you note to yourself.

_____

_____

_____

_____

_____

Write about a "tedious" chore around the house which actually makes you feel happy.

_____

_____

_____

_____

_____

_____

How do children make the world a happier place?

_____

_____

_____

_____

_____

_____

What things do you get to have because of the country you live in that others might not have?

_____

_____

_____

_____

_____

_____

Is there an app on your phone that adds value to your life?

_____

_____

_____

_____

_____

What are some of your favorite things about your town, city or state?

_____

_____

_____

_____

_____

What has improved in your life over the last year?

_____

_____

_____

_____

_____

"When we focus on our gratitude, the tide of disappointment goes out and the tide of love rushes in."

Kristin Armstrong

Name something that comes easily to you and is challenging for others.

_____
_____
_____
_____
_____
_____

Who is a coworker or colleague you appreciate, and why?

_____
_____
_____
_____
_____
_____

Who is someone who has been a positive in your life this week? What is the top thing you would thank them for?

_____
_____
_____
_____
_____
_____

When do you feel most content? How is contentedness a positive in your life?

_____

_____

_____

_____

_____

_____

What is your favorite color and why does it make you happy?

_____

_____

_____

_____

_____

_____

What is a drink you love and why?

_____

_____

_____

_____

_____

_____

Who is someone who has stood up for you in your life?

_____

_____

_____

_____

_____

List three things that bring you comfort during difficult times.

_____

_____

_____

_____

_____

Who is someone who really listens when you talk and how does that affect you?

_____

_____

_____

_____

_____

_____

Reflect on a time when you felt proud of your actions.

_____

_____

_____

_____

_____

_____

What is a place in your community you are thankful for?

_____

_____

_____

_____

_____

Who is someone who takes care of something for you? Hairstylist, garbage man, etc?

_____

_____

_____

_____

_____

_____

List some ways the resiliency of the human spirit has positively affected your life.

_____

_____

_____

_____

_____

Write about a time when you faced your fears and grew stronger.

_____

_____

_____

_____

_____

What is a stressor you are grateful to have put behind you?

_____

_____

_____

_____

_____

_____

How has the freedom to be yourself been a blessing in your life?

_____

_____

_____

_____

_____

_____

Share a recent conversation that made you feel heard and understood.

_____

_____

_____

_____

_____

_____

How many of your basic needs have been met today?

_____

_____

_____

_____

_____

_____

Each day offers you a new start. Write some ways that can be a good thing in your life.

_____

_____

_____

_____

_____

_____

Reflect on a time when you felt proud of your cultural heritage.

_____

_____

_____

_____

_____

_____

What is something enjoyable that you get to experience everyday that you have come to take for granted?

_____

_____

_____

_____

_____

_____

What are some great choices you have made that have led to great outcomes?

_____

_____

_____

_____

_____

_____

What is an aspect of your daily routine that you are grateful for?

_____

_____

_____

_____

_____

What about today has been better than yesterday?

_____

_____

_____

_____

_____

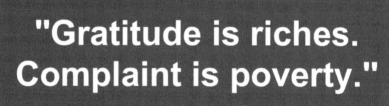

"Gratitude is riches.
Complaint is poverty."

Doris Day

How can you make even a small difference in the world? Your actions can make difference.

_____

_____

_____

_____

_____

_____

What is something that was hard to do but you did it anyway?

_____

_____

_____

_____

_____

_____

What is an aspect of your personality that you are grateful for?

_____

_____

_____

_____

_____

_____

How is the simple ability of breathing a gift?

_____

_____

_____

_____

_____

_____

Who is one person you can't stand? Now write down anything you can learn from them being in your life.

_____

_____

_____

_____

_____

_____

Express gratitude for your eyes and what they allow you to see.

_____

_____

_____

_____

_____

_____

How have your personal beliefs lifted you in times of difficulty?

_____

_____

_____

_____

_____

_____

Reflect on a past disappointment that led to growth.

_____

_____

_____

_____

_____

_____

Express gratitdue for your ears and what they allow you to hear.

_____

_____

_____

_____

_____

_____

Write a grateful thought about someone whose job it is to protect you (firefighter, military personnel).

_____

_____

_____

_____

_____

List three things about your job that you are grateful for.

_____

_____

_____

_____

_____

Express gratitude for your brain and everything that it does for you/allows you to do.

_____

_____

_____

_____

_____

When is a time that your body healed itself?

_____

_____

_____

_____

_____

_____

Name one thing/person that makes your life more exciting?

_____

_____

_____

_____

_____

_____

Express gratitude for your nose and what it allows you to smell.

_____

_____

_____

_____

_____

_____

How has techonology allowed you to stay connected with people?

_____

_____

_____

_____

_____

What are some things you like about your family?

_____

_____

_____

_____

_____

What is an aspect of your upbringing for which you feel grateful?

_____

_____

_____

_____

_____

What equipment do you use at work or around the home that makes your life easier?

_____

_____

_____

_____

_____

_____

Describe a way you have grown closer to a family member.

_____

_____

_____

_____

_____

_____

What are simple activities that bring more positivity into your day? Express gratitude for these.

_____

_____

_____

_____

_____

_____

We can even be grateful for furniture. Identify one piece of furniture that makes a difference in your life.

_____

_____

_____

_____

_____

_____

What is your favorite meal and why are you grateful for it?

_____

_____

_____

_____

_____

_____

What enexpected encounter or event has significantly changed the course of your life for the better?

_____

_____

_____

_____

_____

_____

Write thanks for people who work to make the world a better place. (Scientists, doctors, teachers, etc.)

_____

_____

_____

_____

_____

_____

Write about something positive that happened to you recently that made you feel more fortunate.

_____

_____

_____

_____

_____

What is something you have listened to that has moved or inspired you?

_____

_____

_____

_____

_____

_____

"Enjoy the little things,
for one day you may
look back and realize
they were the big
things."

Robert Brault

Think of someone who is really optimistic. What do you appreciate about their optimism?

_____

_____

_____

_____

_____

_____

What is your favorite thing to do in your free time?

_____

_____

_____

_____

_____

_____

What are you optimistic about? How does optimism improve your life?

_____

_____

_____

_____

_____

_____

Take a moment to recall a time when you were very thorough and got an awesome result.

_____
_____
_____
_____
_____

Share a moment when you felt a profound sense of freedom.

_____
_____
_____
_____
_____

What is gift that brought you joy to receive?

_____
_____
_____
_____
_____
_____

When you are feeling scared, what reminds you that things will be OK?

_____

_____

_____

_____

_____

_____

Write about a fun game you enjoy.

_____

_____

_____

_____

_____

_____

What is a gift that brought you joy to give?

_____

_____

_____

_____

_____

_____

If you were to start feeling insecure, who would you turn to for help? What do you love about that person?

_____

_____

_____

_____

_____

What is the funniest video you have watched recently?

_____

_____

_____

_____

_____

What is something about each of your siblings that you are grateful for?

_____

_____

_____

_____

_____

_____

When has life exceeded your expectations?

_____

_____

_____

_____

_____

_____

What is one thing you are looking forward to experiencing in the future?

_____

_____

_____

_____

_____

_____

What is something about each of your parents that you are grateful for?

_____

_____

_____

_____

_____

_____

**Who is the most compassionate person you know?
What else do you love about them?**

_____

_____

_____

_____

_____

**What is one material possession you are grateful
for that helps you give back to others?**

_____

_____

_____

_____

_____

**What are some things about your grandparents that
you are grateful for?**

_____

_____

_____

_____

_____

_____

Think of something that you came to accept overtime. What has that acceptance shown you?

_____

_____

_____

_____

_____

_____

List three goals you have achieved in your lifetime.

_____

_____

_____

_____

_____

_____

Express gratitude for an ancestor, great-grandparent or further past, positively affected your life.

_____

_____

_____

_____

_____

_____

Think back on a time when things felt fair. What did you appreciate about that time?

_____
_____
_____
_____
_____

What is one thing that is good in the world?

_____
_____
_____
_____
_____

What is a food that is nestolgic for you or evokes positive memories of a loved one?

_____
_____
_____
_____
_____

What do you love about feeling empathy?

_____

_____

_____

_____

_____

_____

What is a moment when you felt overwhelmed with gratitude?

_____

_____

_____

_____

_____

_____

What is a joke that makes you giggle? Laughter is something to be grateful for.

_____

_____

_____

_____

_____

_____

"He is a wise man who does not grieve for the things which he has not, but rejoices for those which he has."

Epictetus

Who is the most loving person you know? How does it feel to be around this person?

_____

_____

_____

_____

_____

_____

What is one thing that helps you feel grounded during busy or turbulent times?

_____

_____

_____

_____

_____

Think about a part of your body that you don't always like. Find something about that to be grateful for.

_____

_____

_____

_____

_____

_____

In what ways do you respect yourself?

_____
_____
_____
_____
_____
_____

Express gratitude for how you have grown and developed through the years.

_____
_____
_____
_____
_____
_____

What was a childhood toy you loved growing up? Write why you are grateful for that toy.

_____
_____
_____
_____
_____
_____

What does vulnerability mean to you? How has vulneralbility blessed you?

_____

_____

_____

_____

_____

_____

Share a personal habit that has improved your life.

_____

_____

_____

_____

_____

_____

What is a song that has comforted you in a difficult time?

_____

_____

_____

_____

_____

_____

Have you ever felt misunderstood? In what ways did those experiences help you to understand yourself?

_____

_____

_____

_____

_____

_____

Reflect through the week and write about moments that made you happy.

_____

_____

_____

_____

_____

What do you like about evening?

_____

_____

_____

_____

_____

_____

What has grief shown you about love? Take a moment to express gratitude for the emotion of grief.

_____

_____

_____

_____

_____

_____

What is one thing you are grateful for that helps you stay active and healthy?

_____

_____

_____

_____

_____

_____

Write about a plant that you appreciate? Trees that give you shade, flowers that beautify the environment, etc.

_____

_____

_____

_____

_____

_____

Think of a time when you were practical and it paid off.

_____

_____

_____

_____

_____

List three aspects of your health you appreciate.

_____

_____

_____

_____

_____

What is a dessert that brings you joy?

_____

_____

_____

_____

_____

What is your favorite grocery store? What do you like about it?

_____

_____

_____

_____

_____

_____

Describe a time when you helped someone in need.

_____

_____

_____

_____

_____

_____

What is something you learned in school that still helps you in your life?

_____

_____

_____

_____

_____

_____

What is your favorite part of your kitchen?

Write about a person who helped you through a tough situation.

What have you recently introduced into my life that's brought me peace, joy, or comfort?

When do you feel worn out in a "good" way?

_____

_____

_____

_____

_____

_____

Reflect on a time when someone offered you an unexpected act of service.

_____

_____

_____

_____

_____

What about your financial situation are you grateful for?

_____

_____

_____

_____

_____

_____

"Appreciation is a wonderful thing. It makes what is excellent in others belong to us as well."

Voltaire

Think of a time when you were assertive. How did your assertiveness pay off?

_____

_____

_____

_____

_____

_____

Write about an unsung hero in your life.

_____

_____

_____

_____

_____

_____

What is something your past self did that you are grateful for today?

_____

_____

_____

_____

_____

_____

Where has discipline served you well?

_____

_____

_____

_____

_____

Write down one highlight of your day and why it's positive for you.

_____

_____

_____

_____

_____

In what ways do you handle a crisis that you are particularly thankful for?

_____

_____

_____

_____

_____

Which boundaries are you so thankful that you set and honored?

_____

_____

_____

_____

_____

_____

List three historical events you are thankful to have learned about.

_____

_____

_____

_____

_____

_____

What do you have today that makes you happy that you did not have a year ago?

_____

_____

_____

_____

_____

_____

What makes you angry? What has that anger taught you about what you need and what you value?

_____

_____

_____

_____

_____

_____

What is a holiday or celebration you look forward to? Why do you look forward to it?

_____

_____

_____

_____

_____

_____

Write a thank you to someone you care about.

_____

_____

_____

_____

_____

_____

What is a truth you know that you are grateful for?

_____

_____

_____

_____

_____

_____

What is something you are grateful for in your home?

_____

_____

_____

_____

_____

_____

What do you appreciate about your current life circumstances?

_____

_____

_____

_____

_____

_____

Who has been your greatest critic? What have they taught you about life?

_____

_____

_____

_____

_____

What top three things/people make your home feel special?

_____

_____

_____

_____

_____

What do you love about sunsets?

_____

_____

_____

_____

_____

Think of a time when you felt curious. What did you learn by exploring your curiosity?

_____

_____

_____

_____

_____

_____

Write about a recent improvement in your lifestyle.

_____

_____

_____

_____

_____

_____

What do you love about the sunrise?

_____

_____

_____

_____

_____

_____

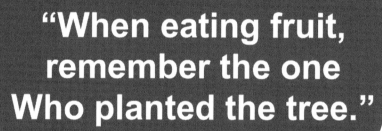

"When eating fruit,
remember the one
Who planted the tree."

Vietnamese Proverb

Think of a time when you were pessimistic but things actually turned out well. What happened?

_____

_____

_____

_____

_____

_____

Who is someone you are grateful for on social media, and why?

_____

_____

_____

_____

_____

Write about someone who supported you in achieving your dreams and why you are grateful for their support.

_____

_____

_____

_____

_____

_____

Who is the most humble person you know? What do you like most about them?

_____

_____

_____

_____

_____

_____

What is a recent technological innovation you are grateful for?

_____

_____

_____

_____

_____

_____

Describe a sentimental possession of yours and why you feel grateful for it.

_____

_____

_____

_____

_____

_____

Think about a misunderstanding in one of your relationships. How did that help you to grow?

_____

_____

_____

_____

_____

_____

What is one thing about the Internet that helps you?

_____

_____

_____

_____

_____

Write about a time when you overcame fear and why you are grateful for overcoming this fear.

_____

_____

_____

_____

_____

_____

When were you really spontaneous? What was amazing about your experience?

_____

_____

_____

_____

_____

Why did you start gratitude journaling? Express gratitude to yourself for taking this step.

_____

_____

_____

_____

_____

Who has taught you about unconditional love in the past or present?

_____

_____

_____

_____

_____

How has your sense of humor helped you?

_____
_____
_____
_____
_____
_____

Share a kind act you did for someone today and what feelings that brought you.

_____
_____
_____
_____
_____

Who or what in your life are you happy to have let go?

_____
_____
_____
_____
_____

Who is the funniest person you know? What makes them funny?

_____

_____

_____

_____

_____

_____

Share a memory of a time when laughter was the best medicine.

_____

_____

_____

_____

_____

_____

What is an event you participated in that made your life better in some way?

_____

_____

_____

_____

_____

_____

Do you ever feel too sensitive? How has your sensitivity paid off?

_____

_____

_____

_____

_____

_____

Who is a leader or public figure you respect, and why? (past or present)

_____

_____

_____

_____

_____

_____

Write a paragraph about one of the best days in your life.

_____

_____

_____

_____

_____

_____

When was the last time you were really generous? What did you enjoy about the experience?

_____

_____

_____

_____

_____

What is a lesson in your life that has helped you?

_____

_____

_____

_____

_____

What are irritations in your life that could use a change in perspective? How can that change your life?

_____

_____

_____

_____

_____

Write about a time when you got really great customer service.

_____

_____

_____

_____

_____

_____

Write about a lesson you learned from a mistake.

_____

_____

_____

_____

_____

_____

Write about 3 groups of people that do not have it as good as you (sick children, homeless people, etc).

_____

_____

_____

_____

_____

_____

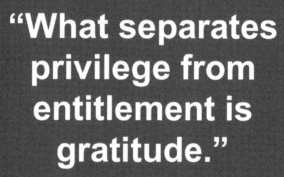

"What separates privilege from entitlement is gratitude."

Brené Brown

Think of a time when you worked really hard on something that failed. What did you learn from that experience?

_____

_____

_____

_____

_____

_____

Write about a place where you find inspiration and creativity.

_____

_____

_____

_____

_____

_____

Write about a time that pure luck or grace has saved you.

_____

_____

_____

_____

_____

_____

What do you care about most? Express gratitude for your caring heart.

_____
_____
_____
_____
_____
_____

List some things that help you feel loved and supported.

_____
_____
_____
_____
_____
_____

What physical characteristics are you most grateful for?

_____
_____
_____
_____
_____
_____

Have you ever lost something, then felt so good finding it? What was it?

_____

_____

_____

_____

_____

_____

Write about a time when you felt loved and cared for.

_____

_____

_____

_____

_____

_____

Express gratitude for something that seems to relax you.

_____

_____

_____

_____

_____

_____

What old, destructive habit have you successfully broken? What is it like without that habit?

_____

_____

_____

_____

_____

What is one thing you are grateful for that helps you manage stress?

_____

_____

_____

_____

_____

What is a place in your home that is comfortable to you?

_____

_____

_____

_____

_____

Who or what has been the biggest pleasant surprise in the past 6 months?

_____

_____

_____

_____

_____

_____

What is a movie or TV show that has had a positive impact on you?

_____

_____

_____

_____

_____

What is a time of day or night that you are most grateful for?

_____

_____

_____

_____

_____

Write gratitude about something you have done to improve your living circumstances?

_____

_____

_____

_____

_____

What is an advancement in medacine you are grateful for?

_____

_____

_____

_____

_____

List five people you care about? Loving others is one of the beauties of being alive.

_____

_____

_____

_____

_____

"We need to learn to want what we have, not to have what we want in order to get stable and steady happiness." Write about what this means to you.

_____

_____

_____

_____

_____

_____

What is one memory or moment you will always cherish?

_____

_____

_____

_____

_____

_____

What is a compliment that you have given or received that brightened your day?

_____

_____

_____

_____

_____

_____

In the past 24 hours, Who has made you smile genuinely? What did she or he do?

_____

_____

_____

_____

_____

Reflect on a positive mentor you have had in your life.

_____

_____

_____

_____

What is the biggest accomplishment in your professional life?

_____

_____

_____

_____

_____

What do you appreciate the most about your partner? Your kids? Your family?

_____

_____

_____

_____

_____

_____

Who is someone you are grateful to have inspired or helped?

_____

_____

_____

_____

_____

What is one something you have learned this week that you are thankful for?

_____

_____

_____

_____

_____

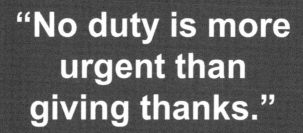

"No duty is more
urgent than
giving thanks."

James Allen

What part of your body you're most appreciative for today?

_____

_____

_____

_____

_____

_____

What is a positive mindset change you have made and how has that influenced your life?

_____

_____

_____

_____

_____

_____

What is the biggest lesson you learned in childhood?

_____

_____

_____

_____

_____

_____

If you're going through a difficult phase, what is the potential silver lining?

_____

_____

_____

_____

_____

List 5 ways that having a mobile phone makes your life easier.

_____

_____

_____

_____

_____

Describe the last time someone helped you solve a problem at work or at home.

_____

_____

_____

_____

_____

Recount the last time you received a gift unexpectedly.

_____

_____

_____

_____

_____

_____

What do you love most about the time you are living in?

_____

_____

_____

_____

_____

_____

If you are single, what is your favorite part about being single? Or if you are married, what is your favorite part about being married?

_____

_____

_____

_____

_____

_____

Describe a situation when you forgave someone. How did you feel?

_____

_____

_____

_____

_____

Name a song that makes you feel joyful and why.

_____

_____

_____

_____

_____

What is a major lesson that you learned from your employment, past or present?

_____

_____

_____

_____

_____

What is your favorite popular music and why do you appreciate it?

_____

_____

_____

_____

_____

_____

Describe a time when you found solace in music.

_____

_____

_____

_____

_____

_____

What is one lesson you learn from rude people? There are reasons to be grateful for all kinds of people.

_____

_____

_____

_____

_____

_____

What is a time when you enjoyed being creative?

_____

_____

_____

_____

_____

Name three things you are thankful for in nature.

_____

_____

_____

_____

_____

What are a few ways you can appreciate your health whenever you are sick?

_____

_____

_____

_____

_____

Make a list of ten ways you could express your thankfulness to others in the next 24 to 48 hours.

_____

_____

_____

_____

_____

_____

Write about an element of nature that fascinates you.

_____

_____

_____

_____

_____

_____

Who has forgiven you for a mistake you have made in the past?

_____

_____

_____

_____

_____

_____

Write a description of your favorite sound. When you hear it, where in your body do you feel it the most?

Share a recent moment when you felt deeply connected with nature.

What is something positive you can learn from one of your less-liked qualities? (i.e. Being anxious means you're really good at planning things out.)

Give an example of your favorite flavor or taste.

_____

_____

_____

_____

_____

_____

Who is a neighbor or community member you appreciate, and why?

_____

_____

_____

_____

_____

_____

Describe a recent time when you truly felt at peace.

_____

_____

_____

_____

_____

_____

Describe a misunderstanding with a loved one that's been resolved. How did you feel when all was forgiven?

_____

_____

_____

_____

_____

_____

What is something that you can do today that people 30 years ago could not?

_____

_____

_____

_____

_____

What is your favorite bit of wisdom that you like to frequently share with others?

_____

_____

_____

_____

_____

"Gratitude is the ability to experience life as a gift. It liberates us from the prison of self-preoccupation."

John Ortberg

Describe an occasion when you followed an instinct and it turned out well.

_____

_____

_____

_____

_____

Who is someone you are thankful to have met recently, and how did you meet?

_____

_____

_____

_____

_____

What is a small win that you accomplished in the past 24 hours?

_____

_____

_____

_____

_____

Describe a day that did not start well but later, you felt much better. What happened?

_____

_____

_____

_____

_____

_____

Reflect on an opportunity that changed your life for the better.

_____

_____

_____

_____

_____

Describe one thing that you like about your commute?

_____

_____

_____

_____

_____

Describe a period or circumstance when you were brave. Take a moment to appreciate your courage.

_____

_____

_____

_____

_____

Share a happy memory from a family outing.

_____

_____

_____

_____

_____

What is a personal viewpoint that positively defines you as a person?

_____

_____

_____

_____

_____

_____

Can you think of a modest victory you've had in the last 24 hours?

_____

_____

_____

_____

_____

_____

Share a moment when you overcame a challenge.

_____

_____

_____

_____

_____

_____

What is a holiday you enjoy and why?

_____

_____

_____

_____

_____

Which of your interests (or activities) would you miss if you couldn't do them anymore?

_____

_____

_____

_____

_____

What did your parents teach you growing up that made you a better person?

_____

_____

_____

_____

_____

Describe a small, everyday thing that you enjoy with a special person in your life.

_____

_____

_____

_____

_____

What was the best gift you have ever given yourself?

_____

_____

_____

_____

_____

_____

What is one material possession you are grateful for that helps you pursue your passions?

_____

_____

_____

_____

_____

What activity do you enjoy most when alone?

_____

_____

_____

_____

_____

What is one aspect of the sun that you are grateful for?

_____

_____

_____

_____

_____

List five appliances in your home that make your life easier.

_____

_____

_____

_____

_____

What activity do you enjoy when with others?

_____

_____

_____

_____

_____

_____

Who is someone you cannot imagine living without? Why do you feel this way?

_____

_____

_____

_____

_____

_____

What are some things you love about your personal style and clothing choices?

_____

_____

_____

_____

_____

_____

What makes you happy when you are feeling down?

_____

_____

_____

_____

_____

_____

What is your favorite word in your native language and why?

_____

_____

_____

_____

_____

_____

Pick a random photo, recollect the memory attached to that photo and write about why you are grateful for that memory.

_____

_____

_____

_____

_____

What freedoms are you most grateful for?

_____

_____

_____

_____

_____

_____

"The heart that gives thanks is a happy one, for we cannot feel thankful and unhappy at the same time."

Douglas Wood

What costs less than $1.00 that you are grateful for and why?

_____

_____

_____

_____

_____

Who is a stranger you met briefly but will never forget?

_____

_____

_____

_____

_____

What is your favorite emotion to feel? Why are you grateful for that emotion?

_____

_____

_____

_____

_____

What are three things you like about the weekends?

_____

_____

_____

_____

_____

_____

List three people who have positively impacted your life.

_____

_____

_____

_____

_____

What makes you happy to be alive?

_____

_____

_____

_____

_____

What do you like about mornings?

_____

_____

_____

_____

_____

_____

How does practicing gratitude impact your thoughts?

_____

_____

_____

_____

_____

_____

What was your favorite game to play as a child?

_____

_____

_____

_____

_____

_____

Reflect on a time you felt proud of a creative project. Why do you appreciate creativity?

_____

_____

_____

_____

_____

_____

What privileges do you enjoy that others might not?

_____

_____

_____

_____

_____

_____

What was the best job you had as a teen or young adult?

_____

_____

_____

_____

_____

_____

Share a favorite memory from a family gathering.

_____
_____
_____
_____
_____

Choose a public service (library, education, etc.) you are grateful for and write a paragraph about it.

_____
_____
_____
_____
_____

Which birthday was your best so far? Why?

_____
_____
_____
_____
_____

Write about a time you felt proud of your character.

_____
_____
_____
_____
_____
_____

What is one material possession you are grateful for that reminds me of a special person or place?

_____
_____
_____
_____
_____

Name three everyday objects that you are grateful for.

_____
_____
_____
_____
_____
_____

Write about one of your favorite subjects in school, past or present?

_____

_____

_____

_____

_____

Who is someone you admire for their resilience, and why?

_____

_____

_____

_____

_____

Name three unique things you are grateful for from this last year.

_____

_____

_____

_____

_____

What are three values or virtues that you appreciate and why.

_____

_____

_____

_____

_____

_____

Write about your favorite season and what you like about it.

_____

_____

_____

_____

_____

_____

What brings you gratitude with the passing of time? (Something you notice more than you used to.)

_____

_____

_____

_____

_____

_____

What's a project or task you completed successfully?

_____

_____

_____

_____

_____

What is one thing that enriches your mental/emotional health?

_____

_____

_____

_____

_____

What self-discovery have you made in the last year that you are thankful for?

_____

_____

_____

_____

_____

"It's a funny thing about life, once you begin to take note of the things you are grateful for, you begin to lose sight of the things that you lack."

Germany Kent

Write about a book, podcast, etc that has opened your mind to new ideas.

_____

_____

_____

_____

_____

Write about a place that brings you a sense of serenity.

_____

_____

_____

_____

_____

What food did you eat today? Take a moment to share gratitude for the food and water that sustains you.

_____

_____

_____

_____

_____

Write about a meal shared with loved ones.

_____

_____

_____

_____

_____

_____

Share a kind gesture you witnessed today or recently.

_____

_____

_____

_____

_____

_____

Where does your food come from? Take a moment to be grateful for those who help grow, ship, prepare food.

_____

_____

_____

_____

_____

_____

Describe a time when you felt supported by friends and/or loved ones.

_____

_____

_____

_____

_____

Write about a beautiful sight you saw today.

_____

_____

_____

_____

_____

What is a guilty pleasure you are thankful for?

_____

_____

_____

_____

_____

Bring into mind a situation that is currently difficult. List three ways you could be grateful for the difficulty.

_____

_____

_____

_____

_____

_____

List three simple pleasures that bring you happiness.

_____

_____

_____

_____

_____

_____

Describe something beautiful that is outside of your window.

_____

_____

_____

_____

_____

_____

What is a favorite piece of art or creativty that brings you joy?

_____

_____

_____

_____

_____

What is one thing you are grateful for that helps you get a good night's sleep?

_____

_____

_____

_____

_____

Name a creative art that brings you joy. (theater, music, painting, literature, etc.) Why?

_____

_____

_____

_____

_____

Who is a classmate/teammate/co-worker/individual you are grateful to have collaborated with?

_____

_____

_____

_____

_____

_____

Look around you and find something that you can feel grateful for, no matter how small.

_____

_____

_____

_____

_____

What do you like about afternoon time?

_____

_____

_____

_____

_____

What is a personal strength you are thankful for in challenging times?

_____

_____

_____

_____

_____

_____

What is a scent or fragrance that evokes positive memories for you?

_____

_____

_____

_____

_____

_____

When were you proud of yourself for getting outside of your comfort zone?

_____

_____

_____

_____

_____

_____

Reflect on a time where you felt grateful for your education.

_____

_____

_____

_____

_____

_____

Name five things that make you smile. Reflect on how these affect your mood.

_____

_____

_____

_____

_____

_____

What is your favorite sight in the entire world?

_____

_____

_____

_____

_____

_____

List three things about a new year that you appreciate.

_____

_____

_____

_____

_____

_____

End of Year Gratitude

List 31 Things to Be Grateful for From This Past Year

1 2 3 4 5 6 7 8 9 10 11 12 13 14 15 16 17 18 19 20 21 22 23 24 25 26 27 28 29 30 31

ADDITIONAL
ACTIVITIES

Gratitude Jar

A gratitude jar is a place where you can collect your reasons to be grateful. Consider writing what you are grateful for each day on strips of paper, place the papers in the jar and visually see how much you are grateful for each year. At the end of each month, draw out and read a couple of the strips of paper.

Why You Are Grateful

In this exercise you're going to get more specific about why you feel grateful for a particular thing. Thinking deeply about the reasons why we are thankful can make us feel more optimistic, aware and connected.

Write one thing for which you are grateful:

Now explain in detail 5 different reasons why you chose this:

1.

2.

3.

4.

5.

Gratitude Reflection

Reflective meditation can help with your gratitude practice. By spending time mindfully aware, learning to just notice what is going on and allowing thoughts and feelings to come and go, you can cultivate a true sense of what it is that makes you feel thankful.

Sit in a comfortable position. Take some deep, breaths to relax yourself. Gently become aware of everything you can smell, taste, touch, see, and hear.
As you notice, say to yourself: "For this, I am grateful."

Now, think about the people and the loved ones in your life.
Again, say to yourself, "For this, I am grateful."

Next, focus on yourself. Think about your strengths and how you are able to learn and overcome challenges.
Say to yourself: "For this, I am grateful."

Last of all, consider how life is a gift. Remind yourself how you live in a time in which you can be healthy, supported and strong.
Say to yourself: "For this, I am grateful."

Gratitude Collage

Add pictures of all the things that make you feel grateful so that you can visualize your gratitude.

Gratitude Rock

A gratitude rock is a small rock that you decorate with a word, phrase, or design that is calming and reminds you to be grateful. How to make and use a gratitude rock:

1. Choose any small rock that fits in your pocket or on your desk.

2. Decorate it with a word, phrase, or design that is calming and reminds you to be grateful.

3. Carry it with you and whenever you feel the rock, take a few repeat your word or phrase.

Gratitude Letter

Writing a gratitude letter to a person you are grateful to have in your life can be a very powerful experience. Choose someone who is important to you and hand write a letter to how they have made an impact on your life and describe in detail why you are grateful to them.

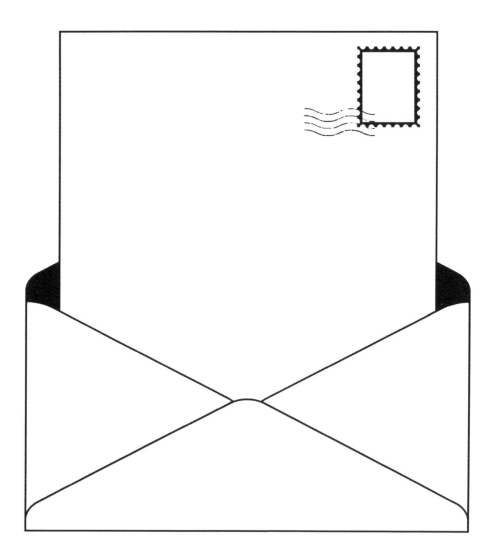

A Gratitude Walk

Take a Gratitude Walk. Go outside into nature and as you walk, closely observe all the things you experience around you. Feel grateful for the sights, smells and sounds that surround you.

Date: Time:

Where I went:

Sights:

Smells:

Sounds:

How this walk made me feel grateful:

Gratitude Charm Bracelet

A charm bracelet can help you to remember all of the things that are important to you and help you feel daily gratitude. Each time that you see or touch your charm bracelet you'll be reminded of how much you have and feel grateful. Some ideas might include:

- A heart to represent your loved ones
- A paw print for your pet
- A flower for your love of nature
- A number for a significant anniversary
- A symbol for your current profession
- A symbol to show your hobbies
- A passport to show your love of travel

Sketch some ideas for your own gratitude charm bracelet here.

Flip Negative Thoughts

This gratitude exercise involves flipping a negative thought into a positive one. By using the phrase, "Yes, and..." you can build on the original thought and turn it around into something more positive. So, every time you find yourself thinking or about to say something negative, stop and try saying "Yes, and..." to try to flip the negative thought. This enables you to find the positive in the negative and feel more grateful about the experience or situation. Here are some examples:

"I'm going to miss the party as I'm ill."
"Yes, and I can get comfy in bed and watch Netflix."

"My friends have cancelled our weekend away."
"Yes, and I can now spend some special time with my brother."

"I didn't get the job I interviewed for."
"Yes, and I can use what I learned at the interview to be better at the next one."

"That business idea didn't work."
"Yes, and I can use what I learned to help my next business."

Write your negative thought here:

And flip it into a positive thought here:

Gratitude By Category

Our lives are multi-faceted. This gives us many categories of things to be grateful for. Consider how grateful you are for each of the areas of your life and write your thoughts in the boxes below

FAMILY & FRIENDS	RECREATION

SPIRITUALITY	FINANCES

PERSONAL GROWTH	BUSINESS & CAREER

HEALTH & FITNESS	RELATIONSHIPS

Gratitude Affirmations

Write down a few gratitude affirmations and repeat them to yourself each day. For example, you could say "I am grateful for my health," "I am grateful for my family and friends," or "I am grateful for the opportunity to live my life."

I am grateful for my health.

I am grateful for my friends and family

I am grateful for the opportunity to live my life.

Acts of Service

Do something nice for someone else. When you do something nice for someone else, it can help you to feel more grateful for the things you have. This could be something small, like giving someone a compliment, or something bigger, like volunteering your time.

Thank You!

Thank you so much for choosing this gratitude journal!
I hope that it has helped you develop your very own
valuable gratitude practice.

Made in the USA
Las Vegas, NV
21 January 2024

84690852R00087